Presented To:

_____

From:

_____

YOUR LOVED ONE IS ILL...
SO NOW WHAT?

*Devotionals for those that
care for the chronically ill*

a devotional collection by

Shelly Benoit Hendricks

Medical Warning and Disclaimer

The information provided in this book is for educational purposes only. Information found within this book is general and cannot address your individual needs. This book is not meant to be used, nor should it be used, to diagnose or treat any medical condition. Before using any information found in this book you should consult with your own physician. For diagnosis or treatment of any medical problem, consult your own physician. The publisher and author are not responsible for any specific health or allergy needs that may require medical supervision and are not liable for any damages or negative consequences from any treatment, action, application or preparation, to any person reading or following the information in this book.

Scripture quotations are taken from the Holy Bible, New Living Translation, copyright ©1996, 2004, 2007, 2013 by Tyndale House Foundation. Used by permission of Tyndale House Publishers, Inc., Carol Stream, Illinois 60188. All rights reserved.

All rights reserved. No part of this publication may be reproduced, stored in a retrieval system, or transmitted, in any form or by any other means, electronic, mechanical photocopying, recording, or otherwise, without prior written permission from the publisher.

Copyright © 2015 Shelly Hendricks

Book and Cover design by Brian Hendricks
Cover / Text photo © Pixabay.com, Bessie (Amazing)
Back Cover photo © Brian Hendricks (Shelly's Portrait)

Renewed Daily Publishing
3761 Newcastle Drive
Sulphur, LA 70663

ISBN-10: 069254979X
ISBN-13: 978-0692549797

CONTENTS

Introduction vii
Lay Down Your Machete 1
What You Should Know 3
No Comparisons, Please 7
A Prayer for a Hard Day 11
Just One Minute 13
The Importance of You 15
Gift Ideas 19
The Giver 25
The Twelve 29
Those Who Love Us 33
Please Stop Saying... 37
Please Start Saying... 41

INTRODUCTION

It is estimated that nearly 1 in 2 people live with a chronic condition. About 96% of those people are suffering silently with invisible illnesses. 75% of marriages impacted by chronic illness end in divorce.

The first statistic became personal for me in the fall of 2009, when I began to experience alarming and mysterious symptoms such as numbness and vision issues.

The following three years were spent seeing a myriad of specialists and ruling out illnesses I had never even heard of... only to leave me doubting my sanity as my illness remained undiagnosed.

Those years were frightening and hopelessness quickly settled in. I continued to cling to God, but some of that clinging came through anger and fear. Slowly but surely, everything I believed about my life and my faith and my value were challenged and stripped away.

The day before Thanksgiving, I received my long-awaited diagnosis. It took about thirty minutes to realize that this was only the first scary step into an entirely new life. My illness is Intracranial Hypertension, also known as Pseudotumor Cerebri. It is a rare neurological disease in which the cerebral spinal fluid is overproduced and does not drain properly. As a result, my brain is under constant high pressure. The symptoms are the same as with a brain tumor, but the tumor is not actually there.

The January following my diagnosis, I had my first brain surgery, during which a shunt was placed inside my brain in order to aid the draining of spinal fluid.

I have now had two brain surgeries, as my first shunt malfunctioned and had to be replaced two years after the first was installed.

I know what it's like to wake up one day and have your life never be the same again, from that point on. I know what it's like to believe I cannot get through this. Just this year, doctors also decided that I have a yet-unnamed neuro degenerative disease. Apparently, all those years of blaming my Intracranial Hypertension for my deteriorating condition were misplaced. That's how chronic illness is sometimes... a constant starting over.

More than this, my family and my marriage and my friendships have all been deeply impacted by the onset of a chronic illness and the subsequent disabilities. Without the willingness to allow changes and embrace newness, these relationships would not have withstood the changes. As it is, some did not survive.

I want to walk with you through the first shocking and confusing days after a chronic illness onset. I want to hold your hand and cry with you. I want to nod when you talk about how hard it is. I want to point you back to God and share the tips that have helped me to make it this far.

You are not alone. This book looks at the raw terror of chronic illness and bravely helps you to put one foot in front of the other, prayerfully right alongside your loved one. These devotionals are honest and real and hopeful, but not in a contrived way.

Are you ready to face this with your God and a friend? I'm right here with you, every step of the way. Let's begin, shall we?

*invisibleillnessweek.com

LAY DOWN YOUR MACHETE

> I will lead blind Israel down a new path, guiding them along an unfamiliar way. I will brighten the darkness before them and smooth out the road ahead of them. Yes, I will indeed do these things; I will not forsake them.
> (Isaiah 42:16, NLT)

I've hacked. Oh, how I've hacked. I've whacked and sweated as I swung my arm with determination. I've cut down walls of vines that seemed impenetrable. I've been slowed by larger plants and stems, stands of bamboo... but not stopped, never stopped.

I've cut this path long enough to suspect it's leading right to a cliff. That or a stone wall dead end. My arms are screaming for relief, there's no end in sight, and I'm exhausted.

Besides, God is able to make a way in rugged places. It's His promise. It's what He does.

Stubborn pride and surety of my own mind and skills has kept me going. Oh, yes, I've leaned on my own self so hard I have dents.

Have you?

Can I encourage you today, as I'm encouraging myself?

It's time... past time...

Lay down your machete.

Dear Lord,
I give up. And it feels so nice to rest in Your expert care. Thank You.
In Jesus' Name, Amen...

LET'S GO DEEPER:

1. What problems have you been hacking through on your path as caretaker?

_____
_____
_____
_____

2. How does this affect your energy level?

_____
_____
_____

3. Write here a verse that helps when you feel overwhelmed.

_____
_____
_____
_____

4. What is one thing you can do, today, to begin to share the load or lay it at Jesus' feet?

_____
_____
_____
_____

WHAT YOU SHOULD KNOW

Just as our bodies have many parts and each
part has a special function, so it is with
Christ's body. We are many parts of one body,
and we all belong to each other.
(Romans 12:4-5, NLT)

Okay, maybe "know" is too small of a word... the word should be "understand". Yes? Following are ten things you should understand:

#10 – We know exactly how long we've been out. We do not need reminding about how often we are "sick". I know this will shock some people, but the impression that anyone's immune system is under their control is an illusion. Hopefully, you live on the sunny side of that illusion. Take it from us on the harsher side... we can not help it.

#9 – We have tried bleach. We have aired out our homes. We wash our hands regularly. And we have tried every single search result "fix" that comes around the pike for our condition. So have our doctors. We are insulted by life enough without having to hear what you think we are not doing to help ourselves. Trust us, we're doing it.

#8 – We miss life. You know, real life. We miss being busy and care taking and "going out". Heck, we miss things like walking across the room without thinking about it. We know you are busy, and we are very glad that you can be. Please take a little time, even two minutes, out of your day every once in a while to connect with us. We feel forgotten. A phone call, an e-mail, a card, or oh-my-goodness a short visit… those things can sustain us for weeks and truly make us feel like we are remembered and loved. No one likes to feel like they are only important when they have something to physically contribute, or when they can keep up.

#7 – Although we truly appreciate you offering to help us, an offer like, "Call me if you need anything," is most often going to go unused. Most of us have too much pride and sincerely don't want to be a burden to anyone. We very rarely ask for help. We do, however, appreciate when you say things like, "I'm bringing supper tomorrow night! Take the night off! I'll be there at 5:30; does your family like spaghetti?" or "I'm running by the store on my way home. What can I pick up for you? You can pay me when I get there with your items. It's on my way." You get the picture. Offer specific help at a specific time. Don't wait for us to call, because we likely never will. Our bad, and we're working on it. We appreciate your patience.

#6 – This is hard, living like this. We long to hold down a full-time job. We'd love to run a marathon or be able to drive or even scrub a toilet! Please don't think or act like we are on a vacation or have so much free time. Believe me when I tell you that being sick is work. It is awful and a grief for us.

#5 – We will most likely never ask you to do things differently. We will instead drop out and become more and more isolated. This especially applies to our families, closest friends, and caretakers. We already feel like we're more trouble than we're worth. Please recognize that "the way things have always been" may not be possible anymore. Please sit down with us and come up with a "new normal" plan and hug us often during this talk. We don't want you to have any losses. We love you and want you have what you need, always.

#4 – If you are sick or running a fever and may be contagious, for goodness sake, please stay home. We already catch every germ within five miles and keep it three times as long as you do. This rule should apply to the workplace, school (because my kids bring your kids' germs home), the grocery store, and even (shocked gasp) church services. God understands, He really does, if you are too sick to attend services. The rest of us thank you.

#3 – Attention please: This illness is forever. No such thing as "get well soon". Please stop being surprised when we are "still" ill when you see us. We always will be. Just because we looked pretty last week does not mean we are suddenly and miraculously cured. Just because you saw us out yesterday does not mean we will be able to get out tomorrow. In fact, it's usually exactly the opposite. Hard to understand? Yes. Yes, it is. For us, too.

#2 – Even though we are home bound or disabled, we still have so much more to offer than our illness. We have interests and hobbies and a sense of humor. We love to catch up and tell stories and laugh. Remember that person we were "before"? We're still that same person inside.

#1 – If there's something you know we can do to help, something that is within our abilities, please include us! Even if it's just to say, "We're having a ladies' day next week. Will you keep that in prayer?" or "If I get you a list of the sick each week, will you prepare cards for the congregation to sign?" We want to help. We love to be included.

Dear Lord,
Help us to hold each other up in love. Remind us to be patient and to consider others more important than ourselves.
In Jesus' Name, Amen...

LET'S GO DEEPER:

1. What suggestions on this list surprised you?

___

2. How will this list change how you treat your chronically ill loved one?

___

3. Write here a verse that helps you to remember to speak in love.

___

4. What is one thing you can do, today, to let your loved one know that they are important, just the way they are?

___

NO COMPARISONS, PLEASE

> The idol makers encourage one another, saying
> to each other, "Be strong!"
> (Isaiah 41:6, NLT)

I'd like to talk a little today about this concept we all seem to have that states that in order to make oneself feel better, one should find someone worse off to consider.

People, I have to tell you, this bothers me. It bothers me deep down where Jesus lives. And I'll give you a few reasons why.

The first reason I don't agree with this stream of thought is that it encourages us to make comparisons. I don't think we're called to do that as Christians. It goes back to weeping with those that weep.

> Be happy with those who are happy,
> and weep with those who weep.
> (Romans 12:15, NLT)

Perhaps my worst fear is that something would happen to my children. Perhaps your worst fear is that something would happen to you, and you would be unable to care for yourself and those you love.

Perhaps another's worst fear is a dread disease that would bring painful death, and yet another's terror is a mental disease that would leave their body healthy while their mind withers.

We could go on like this all day. Do you see what I mean? Let's try something new... let's trust that the one who is doing his best to have us live out our fears knows what those are and will attack each of us with that in mind. We don't all have to share the same fear in order for the fear to be real.

No comparisons, please.

Another reason that I don't like this phrase as a comfort is that thinking of others who are supposedly worse off than we are leaves us feeling like we have no right to grieve. This is not what God expects from us. If we had to keep a smile on at all times, we would be less than human. We would be fake. And we would need a little padded room and nice jacket with shiny buckles.

Let's just see... if I have a tumor, at least it hasn't spread. If I have lost a limb, at least I haven't lost three. If I am paralyzed from the waist down, at least I can still move my arms.

Now let's get even crazier (cause let's face it, health issues can get pretty gnarly)... if I am confined to my home, at least I am not confined to my bed. But if I am confined to my bed, at least I am not paralyzed in my bed. And if I am paralyzed in my bed, at least I am not a vegetable. And here's the kicker... if we follow this through to the end, even those who are kept alive only by machines are at least not dead, right? Right?

It's basically a death spiral of trying desperately to make ourselves or others feel better about their pitiful condition by comparing it to the next level of awful... and each level down is determined strictly from the speaker's list of fears.

NO COMPARISONS, PLEASE

So today, I give each of you permission to grieve your losses. To reconnoiter your troops and take a little time to breathe through your pain. Don't worry about the gal next to you. She is gathering her own courage. Don't consider the guy up the road. He is dealing with his own demons.

No comparisons, please.

There is plenty of room for all of our troubles. It doesn't bring comfort to ourselves or others to be reminded of other suffering people any more than knowing about starving people in other parts of the world makes you want to eat brussel sprouts for supper.

Brussel sprouts still taste nasty. Illness, pain, and disability, in all forms, still crush.

It's okay to acknowledge that... to yourself and to others.

Don't feel like you have to apologize that your loved one's illness stinks (lest we then need to compare the stinky diaper odor to the garbage truck odor to the rotting carcass odor). Don't rush to soothe your aching heart with a quick listing of others whom you see as more tortured than yourself.

Instead, acknowledge your pain and the pain of others. Pray. And if you're a friend struggling for what to say now that I've taken this option off the table, pray. Pray with us, right there in that moment. Say you're sorry that it hurts. Or say nothing at all and simply give a heart-felt hug.

It is what it is, no matter how many other hurting people there are in the world.

No comparisons, please.

Lord Jesus,
You show us mercies in every aspect of Your life.
Help us to lend those same mercies to ourselves.
Help us to extend them to others just as readily.
Keep comparisons far from our heart.
In Jesus' Name, Amen...

LET'S GO DEEPER:

1. What kind of comparisons have you seen your loved one making?

___

2. How about yourself?

___

3. Write here a verse that reminds you that we each have our cross to bear.

___

4. What is one thing you can do, today, to help your loved one express their pain or grief without reproach?

___

A PRAYER FOR A HARD DAY

He also says to the Son, "In the beginning, Lord, you laid the foundation of the earth and made the heavens with your hands. They will perish, but you remain forever. They will wear out like old clothing. You will fold them up like a cloak and discard them like old clothing. But you are always the same; you will live forever."

(Hebrews 1:10-12, NLT)

May my grief not be so loud as to drown out the sound of the song You sing over me.

May my pain not be so strong

as to erase my remembrance of the cross You bore.

May my voice not be so weak

that I can't still sing in joy to You.

Let the words that You have written on my heart

keep it beating through the struggle that is today.

Allow the goodness that is Your mercy

to breach the walls I may put up in despair.

Keep me sane as I swirl in the tide of confusion
that comes from any surrender to the enemy.
Keep me tethered, always reaching
for only You.
In Jesus' Name, Amen...

LET'S GO DEEPER:

1. What areas of your life are the hardest to face?

___

2. How do these areas affect your prayers?

___

3. Write here a verse that helps you to remember that God cares about your burdens.

___

4. What is one thing you can do, today, that is kind to YOU?

___

JUST ONE MINUTE

> That is why we never give up. Though our bodies are dying, our spirits are being renewed every day. For our present troubles are small and won't last very long. Yet they produce for us a glory that vastly outweighs them and will last forever! So we don't look at the troubles we can see now; rather, we fix our gaze on things that cannot be seen. For the things we see now will soon be gone, but the things we cannot see will last forever.
> (2 Corinthians 4:16-18, NLT)

I wanted to tell you about something I do quite often, and you can do it no matter how busy you are. It only takes one minute. Literally. One minute.

When I'm feeling extra lost, or grieving extra hard, and the walls feel like they're closing in, I set my timer. It's on my computer, so it's easy-peasy and very accurate. I close my eyes as I hit the green button. And then I just keep them closed, bow my head, breathe deep and pray. I keep praying until the timer beeps. Sometimes I'm jumping from one thought to another and to my ears it sounds a little scattered. But I trust that the Spirit can get my message across. He promised to, after all.

> And the Holy Spirit helps us in our weakness. For example, we don't know what God wants us to pray for. But the Holy Spirit prays for us with groanings that cannot be expressed in words.
> (Romans 8:26, NLT)

When that timer goes off, the world tries to rush back in. But just one minute is all it takes. To fix my gaze. To anchor my trust. To remind me what matters.

I challenge you today to give yourself just a minute when panic or pain sets in. You might find it's all you need, simply because of the One you spend it with.

Dear Father,
Thank You for hope. Thank You for settling us when nothing else will. We love You.
In Jesus' Name, Amen...

LET'S GO DEEPER:

1. What kind of pressures crowd out your time and make you feel frazzled?

_____
_____
_____

2. How can one minute make a difference to you?

_____
_____
_____

3. Write here a verse that helps you to visualize the Holy Spirit interceding for you.

_____
_____
_____

4. What is one thing you can do, today, to carve a quiet minute out of your day?

_____
_____
_____

THE IMPORTANCE OF YOU

> But Ahaziah's sister Jehosheba, the daughter of King Jehoram, took Ahaziah's infant son, Joash, and stole him away from among the rest of the king's children, who were about to be killed. She put Joash and his nurse in a bedroom. In this way, Jehosheba, wife of Jehoiada the priest and sister of Ahaziah, hid the child so that Athaliah could not murder him.
> (2 Chronicles 22:11, NLT)

Poor Jehosheba. She had to stand by and see so many children slain. Her nieces and her nephews were murdered right before her eyes. Can you relate?

She could only save one, a baby still in need of his nurse. You can reach one, too, and your importance in their life can not be overstated.

If the princess had the frame of mind we have these days, little Joash would have perished. I mean, if you're only one and you can only reach one, what's the point, right? If Jehosheba was focused on her numbers instead of playing her part, no matter how small, Joash would not have been saved.

But her part, you see, was not so small after all. It was huge. Epic.

See, Athaliah was an evil queen and she was determined to wipe out the line of Judah. Wipe. It. Out. The only thing standing between her and success was Jehosheba and baby Joash.

God saved that remnant of the royal line so that we could have a Savior from the prophesied lineage a thousand years later (give or take). Without baby Joash, there could be no baby Jesus.

Today, take your eyes off the numbers. Stop considering yourself too small to make a difference. Do what you can and leave the power of it all to the One who can use it in epic ways you may never even see.

He's using You. Your one tiny drop makes ripples that have eternal consequences. Believe it. You matter.

Amazing God,
Use me. It is my deepest prayer. Use us all. We know that we are never invisible to You.
In Jesus' Name, Amen...

LET'S GO DEEPER:

1. What kind of amazing things did you do today?

_____
_____
_____
_____

2. How did those things make you feel about yourself?

_____
_____
_____
_____

3. Write here a verse that helps you to remember that what you give matters.

_____
_____
_____

4. What is one thing you can do, today, to help you keep your importance in mind?

_____
_____
_____
_____

YOUR LOVED ONE IS ILL... SO NOW WHAT?

GIFT IDEAS

Love each other with genuine affection, and take delight in honoring each other.
(Romans 12:10, NLT)

It's hard, isn't it? It's hard to be the recipient who receives a "get well soon" card when you never will. But sometimes it's even harder to be the one trying to guess what to give in order to be the most sensitive and caring. I hope this list will help with that. Just know that your friendship and love, your time and attention, will be the greatest treasure to your friend or loved one. Thank you for being here. Truly.

1. Know your recipient. Choose something that pertains to their "hobby" or interest. What do they do in their downtime? Many of us have an overabundance of that, and life can feel empty if we do not find or develop an interest that we can do while sitting or laying at home. If they stitch or knit, supplies for that are probably viewed as "extras" and if they have to be bought regularly there may be guilt attached to the purchase. A writer will probably appreciate a journal and pretty pen. Use your imagination, and don't be afraid to ask how they like to spend their time. A reader would probably enjoy an inspirational book, like one from Joni Eareckson Tada. You may even inquire about their favorite authors. Perhaps they enjoy scrap booking or another craft. If you aren't sure about specifics, a gift card to their favorite online hobby store is a perfect idea.

2. Entertainment changes greatly when you become ill. Most has to be found at home, and a lot of it in your pajamas. What does your friend enjoy? If they are a music lover, music CD's or subscription to a music streaming service are great gifts. MP3 players or even headphones are another idea that goes along with this. If your family member is a movie buff, a movie streaming subscription or credit on their favorite new movie service would be a thoughtful gift. Consider including microwave popcorn and hot cocoa or their favorite candy. Perhaps they miss being able to dine out. In that case, gift cards to delivery services or a local pizzeria are a great idea! Perhaps include a candle for the dining table or some funky place mats for enjoying their delivered meal in style.

3. It is such a joy to receive mail when you are homebound. A great gift idea is monthly treats, like "of the month" clubs.... flowers or treats or even something like tea... this gives your loved one something to look forward to coming in the mail regularly. Brighten their lives all year long with one gift.

4. A gift that never gets old and is guaranteed to be used is a gift certificate... speaking for the chronically ill community here, we don't often splurge on ourselves since funds are almost always limited and necessary items are often so expensive. Therefore a gift certificate to a great site that features what would be considered an extravagance or treat to your recipient is the perfect way to make them feel special. You may even want to specify that the money must be used for "non-essentials", so that they know that they are to treat themselves with your gift.

5. If your friend is often home-bound, a wonderful gift idea is something to draw nature to the window they most often sit near. There are bird feeders that attach to a window. Feeders for other animals they may enjoy, a birdbath, sun-catchers... all of these things help to being the joy of nature right into the room with your friend. The simplest nature sightings can literally make your friend's day.

6. You might consider making a donation to your family member's favorite organization. This can be done by shopping in the store of the organization, or through a straight donation in your friend's name. If your pal is an activist or seriously interested in supporting a cure or spreading awareness, this would be a very thoughtful purchase.

7. Any chronically ill individual, regardless of male or female, age, location, or level of ability, will appreciate something cozy. I guarantee it. Now let's step out of the "candle mind-frame" for just a moment here. Some people really love candles. In that case, shop on. However, many chronically ill have allergies to scents or other ingredients and if they receive a candle or bath item from you, they may not be able to use it. When you are shopping for cozy, if you aren't sure of specific things to avoid, think soft and warm more than smell-good. Fuzzy socks, soft blankets, fluffy scarves, extra pillows or cushions. Comfy is key.

8. If you know the correct sizes for your recipient, you may consider getting them comfy clothes or something like a cardigan. We often have trouble controlling our body temperature. Any clothes we choose to wear needs to be flowy and non-binding. Elastic is better than buttons or zippers, as we may not be able to grasp well. Pajamas are always welcome, as are slippers.

9. The gift of pampering is always a welcome gift. Depending on if you are buying for a man or a woman, you may consider gifts such as a spa day, a house cleaning service, a car wash coupon, or a lawn care service. Use your imagination and apply what you know of your recipient. Perhaps these are services you yourself could offer, in which case homemade coupons would be well-received. A gift does not need to be expensive to be treasured. The gift of your time and care are priceless.

10. Last but not least, is there a helpful item you know would make their life easier? Perhaps there is something they truly need, but have been unable to save up to purchase. A wheelchair cushion? Compression gloves? Arthritis shoes? Diabetic socks? A shower chair or handheld shower? Again, if you're not certain what to choose and are uncomfortable asking (or they are uncomfortable answering), a gift card to a favorite store would be welcomed. You can specify how you would like the money to be spent, if they are willing.

Thank you for reading this list. The fact that you are interested and searching means the world to your friend or family member. Trust me on this... it does.

Dear God,
Thank You for each caring soul reading this today. Thank You for their willingness to love when it's hard. Thank You for their willingness to make extra effort to show care. Bless them, Lord.
In Jesus' Name, Amen...

LET'S GO DEEPER:

1. What kind of gifts do you find it hard to shop for?

___

2. How does this affect your gift-giving?

___

3. Write here a verse that helps you to remember that God is the giver of good gifts to His children.

___

4. What is one thing you can do, today, to become more specific in your shopping?

___

YOUR LOVED ONE IS ILL... SO NOW WHAT?

THE GIVER

"You parents—if your children ask for a loaf of bread, do you give them a stone instead? Or if they ask for a fish, do you give them a snake? Of course not! So if you sinful people know how to give good gifts to your children, how much more will your heavenly Father give good gifts to those who ask him." (Matthew 7:9-11, NLT)

Let's play a game today? Are you game? (sorry, I couldn't resist)

Let's choose our story. I think it would be fun to do it from the Bible, that way we can see how it would end.

I'll start.

Hmmm, will I choose to be the prostitute who lives inside the impenetrable walls? Safe but defiled. Surrounded by a people who value only their own pleasures, and tremble only over the name of a God they refuse to bow down and worship. I think not. That life is not for me. Who would choose that life?

On the lookout for a better story to be a part of, I come across a princess. Now that's more like it, right? Life is so handed to me, that even a baby just floats right down the river and into my arms. Pampered, wealthy, in charge. That sounds like much more my speed, right?

God is topsy-turvy, isn't He?

This Father who knows how to give good gifts, He saved that dishonored woman. She alone, out of an entire city, was left standing in the rubble. She was taken in and loved. She was adopted into the family and became such a vital part that she's listed in the genealogy of the Messiah. Take that in for just a minute.

That princess, she raised that child of slaves, and he returned to lay ruin to all that she felt was untouchable. Her life came to nothing, and is only remembered because it was used to showcase the terrible power of a God defied.

I guess I'm not a very good chooser.

How about you? If you play my little game, would you choose any better? Our logic is flawed, isn't it?

The same thing happens in my real life. Today. This very minute. I wonder why I have so much pain. I question why my finances just will not see black. I ask, daily, why God has chosen this for me. How can He name Himself the giver of all good things, and see what I'm going through?

Do you ever wonder?

This life, it isn't a stone. It's living bread.

> Jesus replied, "I am the bread of life. Whoever comes to me will never be hungry again. Whoever believes in me will never be thirsty.
> (John 6:35, NLT)

My vision is so limited. My faith. Whew, does it even add up to mustard-seed-proportions?

> Such things were written in the Scriptures long ago to teach us. And the Scriptures give us hope and encouragement as we wait patiently for God's promises to be fulfilled.
> (Romans 15:4, NLT)

When you read the stories, do you read it through till the end? I'm determined to. Maybe it can shore up my faith. Restore my hope.

Make me a better chooser.

Dear God,
Thank You for a lesson in perspective. Thank You for giving way better gifts than I would ask for.
In Jesus' Name, Amen...

LET'S GO DEEPER:

1. What kind of questions have you been asking God since becoming a caregiver?

___
___
___

2. Do you often wish for a different story?

___
___
___

3. Write here a verse that helps you to remember that God really is the Giver of all good gifts.

___
___
___

4. What is one thing you can do, today, to begin to help both of you to accept your story?

___
___
___

YOUR LOVED ONE IS ILL... SO NOW WHAT?

THE TWELVE

Jesus knew what they were saying, so he said, "Why are you arguing about having no bread? Don't you know or understand even yet? Are your hearts too hard to take it in? 'You have eyes—can't you see? You have ears—can't you hear?' Don't you remember anything at all? When I fed the 5,000 with five loaves of bread, how many baskets of leftovers did you pick up afterward?"
"Twelve," they said.
(Mark 8:17-19, NLT)

Here's the dirty dozen we should really be focusing on as our lives seemingly spin out of control.

Picture it...

A distant shore, crowds stretching as far as the eye can see. Men, women, children. Resting in what shade they can find, splashing their feet in the cool water, edging closer and closer to this Man who held more healing in His words than He held in His hands.

Twelve of the closest friends approach Him as evening draws near. "Send them away," they say, "so they can go and buy food for themselves." The Bible tells us there were 5,000, but that's only the men. The men numbered 5,000. Jesus answered his disciples, "They do not need to go away. You feed them."

Um, yeah. Ooookkkkaaayyy, Jesus. Maybe you've been out in this heat a little too long! They counted up all they had, every morsel they could scrounge up.

Shuffling of feet and maybe a few dramatic eye rolls probably ensued, as they tried to decide which one of them would report that they only had five loaves and two fish.

Can you imagine it?

I feel this way pretty often. Oh, the days when I'm just certain I don't have what it takes. The nights when I fret over how on earth I can keep going.

A lot like those friends with the pitiful lunch pail. Five loaves. For over 5,000 people. People who hadn't eaten for at least that entire day, as evening loomed.

But look at the verse that started this post. After all of those hungry people had eaten their fill, the disciples were sent out among them to collect the broken left-overs. The edges that stomachs were too satisfied to indulge.

Twelve baskets. Twelve. Baskets. Full.

> I pray that from his glorious, unlimited resources he will empower you with inner strength through his Spirit. Then Christ will make his home in your hearts as you trust in him. Your roots will grow down into God's love and keep you strong. And may you have the power to understand, as all God's people should, how wide, how long, how high, and how deep his love is. May you experience the love of Christ, though it is too great to understand fully. Then you will be made complete with all the fullness of life and power that comes from God. Now all glory to God, who is able, through his mighty power at work within us, to accomplish infinitely more than we might ask or think.
> (Ephesians 3:16-20, NLT)

Dear God,
May I ever be aware of the fullness of Your care.
May I ever trust it.
In Jesus' Name, Amen...

LET'S GO DEEPER:

1. Do you ever find yourself worrying over things you've seen God provide before?

_____
_____
_____
_____

2. How does that keep you feeling hopeless?

_____
_____
_____
_____

3. Write here a verse that will remind you that God goes above and beyond what is needed.

_____
_____
_____
_____

4. What is one thing you can do, today, to speak with your loved one about the leftovers?

_____
_____
_____
_____

YOUR LOVED ONE IS ILL... SO NOW WHAT?

THOSE WHO LOVE US

> If I could speak all the languages of earth and of angels, but didn't love others, I would only be a noisy gong or a clanging cymbal. If I had the gift of prophecy, and if I understood all of God's secret plans and possessed all knowledge, and if I had such faith that I could move mountains, but didn't love others, I would be nothing. If I gave everything I have to the poor and even sacrificed my body, I could boast about it; but if I didn't love others, I would have gained nothing.
> (1 Corinthians 13:1-3, NLT)

For all those who worry about the details, who stay up with us when we can't sleep, who demand better when we just lay there and accept less-than-stellar care…

For all of you who stick by instead of turning away, who enjoy the silent tears as much as the carefree laughter, who insist that growth and change are normal instead of mourning that things can't be the way they were…

To every soul who has assured us that our less is actually more, who has given when we have nothing left to offer, who nods with understanding when we whine and complain…

To those who run in while others are racing out, who dig in their heels and refuse to let us go, who tie us to this world with gossamer threads...

There really are no words to express what we feel for you. How much we need you. What we long to be able to give you.

You are a beautiful treasure placed right into our lives by the hands of our Heavenly Father. Thank you for being here, for being you, for just being.

We love you right back. <3

Dear God,

Please help each blessing in my life to feel what a difference they make. Every single day. Thank You for each one.

In Jesus' Name, Amen...

LET'S GO DEEPER:

1. What kind of ways does your loved one let you know that you are wonderful in their lives?

___
___
___
___

2. Write here a verse that helps you to remember that the things you do are done for God's glory.

___
___
___
___

3. What is one thing you can do, today, to begin to allow yourself to feel needed and loved?

_____
_____
_____
_____

YOUR LOVED ONE IS ILL... SO NOW WHAT?

PLEASE STOP SAYING...

So encourage each other and build each other up, just as you are already doing.
(1 Thessalonians 5:11, NLT)

Please stop saying:

"Push Through"

That is a fine premise right up until that moment when you just can't any more. If that moment has not arrived for you, Kudos. The rest of us feel like we must not be trying hard enough when you say this. Or that you think we must not be trying hard enough. I know that's probably far from the truth, but our reality just has no 'push' left and we sure do wish it did.

"I refuse to let..."

This is most often used in conjunction for something you are holding tight to. Same principal applies as above. Those of us who have run out of choices in the matter feel pretty miserable when you say, "I just refuse to let this illness rob me of _____". Okay. We don't really know how to answer that. Perhaps I just didn't refuse hard enough to keep the skill of oh, I don't know, walking? Or making it to church services? Or something I really love like hiking or driving? Again, this statement leaves the impression that we have some say in the loss.

"God won't give you more than you can bear"

This is a lie and a twisting of actual scripture. That scripture says:

> The temptations in your life are no different from what others experience. And God is faithful. He will not allow the temptation to be more than you can stand. When you are tempted, he will show you a way out so that you can endure.
> (1 Corinthians 10:13, NLT)

Seriously. This is more than I can bear. Losing a child is more than a parent can bear. Cancer is more than we can bear. Lots of things this world saddles us with are beyond our endurance. That's why Faith makes such a difference. Trying to navigate all this without the One Person who is able to bear it is just plain nuts.

"It could be worse"

No kidding, Sherlock. Great detective work there. First of all, this depends on who you are and what your fears are. I think we can agree that the enemy knows our fears well enough to hit us where it hurts the most. Maybe what's 'worse' for you isn't necessarily worse for me.

Secondly, this robs people of their right to grieve, to ask for comfort, to lean. Please don't rob them (don't rob me) of this.

It's okay to say nothing. Sometimes your presence means the world to someone who is hurting. A hug is always welcome. I've had friends who cry with me. What a gift.

We need to remove these things from our conversation. Who's with me?

Father in Heaven,

Be with those who are hurting today. Please help my words always and only to build up and share in sorrow.

In Jesus' Name, Amen...

LET'S GO DEEPER:

1. What is something you have said to try and "help" that you later found out does damage?

___

2. How does this list help you to comfort your loved one?

___

3. Write here a verse that helps you to remember that words are powerful.

___

4. What is one thing you can do, today, to show empathy and understanding to your loved one?

___

YOUR LOVED ONE IS ILL... SO NOW WHAT?

PLEASE START SAYING...

> Kind words are like honey—
> sweet to the soul and healthy for the body.
> (Proverbs 16:24, NLT)

We talked about things not to say, and why. Today, let's talk about healing things you should say.

Please start saying:

"I believe you"

For those of us with chronic illness, this is a seldom-heard and oh-so-needed phrase. It's like finding a spring in the desert for us. We will love you forever if you say this and mean it. Seriously.

"I'm sorry it hurts so much"

This is acknowledging that this thing called life is hard. True that. Sometimes it isn't okay and it can't be fixed, but your presence and your acknowledgment can make all the difference. You can literally change or save a life by just making this one statement

"I'll be right there"

Okay, so this is great at face value and if you can make it happen, please do. However, sometimes you can't get there or be there in person. The point of including this statement is to say that if there is something you know you can do, don't wait to be asked. Don't wait to be invited over. Don't wait. Period. Jump in and do or be where you can. It is such a huge blessing.

"Come here"

This one is best wielded with a hug. A long hug that squeezes tight and warm and meaningful. An offer of a shoulder for as long as it takes for the tears to slow and the sobs to recede. The measure of this cannot be overestimated in importance.

I hope you find these comments helpful as you go into a hurting world. Everyone's suffering in one way or another, so give grace freely and sprinkle love around like fairy dust. You might be surprised at who can fly after all.

Father in Heaven,

Be with those who are reaching out to the hurting today. Bless them tenfold for each grace they offer.

In Jesus' Name, Amen...

LET'S GO DEEPER:

1. What is something you were surprised to find on this list?

_____
_____
_____
_____

2. How does this list help you to comfort your loved one?

_____
_____
_____
_____

3. Write here a verse that helps you to remember that words are powerful.

_____
_____
_____
_____

4. What is one thing you can do, today, to show empathy and understanding to your loved one?

_____
_____
_____
_____

YOUR LOVED ONE IS ILL... SO NOW WHAT?

www.ingramcontent.com/pod-product-compliance
Lightning Source LLC
Chambersburg PA
CBHW051800230426
43670CB00012B/2375